METAVERSE FOR NEWBIE

EXPLORING THE BOUNDARIES OF VIRTUAL REALITY

ANURAG SAXENA

This book is dedicated to the pioneers of the Metaverse. To those who have taken the first steps towards creating a platform for all to explore, collaborate and create in a shared digital space. To those who have been brave enough to innovate, challenge the status quo and to strive for a more immersive, interconnected future. Your determination and creativity have been the foundation for our collective progress and will continue to guide future generations. We thank you.

To the adventurers, the dreamers, the creators, the innovators and the visionaries who will shape the future of the Metaverse. We thank you for your courage to explore and build something greater than ourselves. We thank you for your dedication to advancing the boundaries of technology and for your tireless effort to imagine a better world.

Finally, to all those who will one day join us in the Metaverse. We hope this book can serve as a useful guide and a source of inspiration as you set out on your own journey. May you always remember that anything is possible in the virtual world, and that with the right passion and dedication, you can make the Metaverse your own. With sincere appreciation and gratitude,

Contents

Foreword

This is the first book to address the incredible potential of the Metaverse, a digital environment where users can interact, create, and explore in ways never before possible. This book, "Metaverse Manifesto," explores the implications of this new technology and its influence on the world.

The Metaverse is an exciting new technology that can be used to create 3D virtual worlds, allowing users to connect and collaborate with each other in a virtual space. This technology has the potential to revolutionize the way we interact, create, and explore.

This book is an exploration of the Metaverse and its implications. It covers the basics of the technology and its potential applications, as well as the social and legal issues that need to be addressed. It is intended to be a starting point for those interested in the Metaverse, and to provide a framework for further exploration and discussion. The Metaverse is a powerful technology that can shape the future of our society. I am excited to see what the future brings, and I hope this book serves as a valuable resource in that journey.

Sincerely,
Anurag Saxena

Preface

The Metaverse Manifesto is a manifesto that outlines the vision of a world in which the physical and digital realms are seamlessly integrated. It is a vision of the future that is being built today, where the boundaries between the physical and digital worlds are becoming increasingly blurred.

The Metaverse Manifesto is an effort to articulate the principles that will guide the development of this new reality. It is a vision that seeks to create an open, interconnected, and equitable digital world that will enable people to collaborate, innovate, and create in new and powerful ways.

The Metaverse Manifesto is an invitation to anyone interested in the potential of the digital realm to join in the effort to create a better, more equitable future. It is a call to action to all who care about the future of our digital world to come together and create a shared vision of that future.

We invite you to join us in our quest to build a better Metaverse. We invite you to explore the Manifesto and join us in the effort to create an open, equitable and interconnected digital world.

Thank you for joining us on this journey. Together, we can create a better future.

Acknowledgements

First and foremost, I would like to thank those who have generously supported me in the creation of this book.
My family, thank you for your patience and understanding during the long hours of writing and research. Your words of encouragement and support pushed me to keep going.

To my friends, thank you for believing in me and for your enthusiasm and enthusiasm to read the finished product. Your support was invaluable.

To my colleagues, thank you for your expertise and opinion. Your insights were instrumental in shaping of this work.

Finally, to all of the people who have contributed to the Metaverse Manifesto in any capacity, thank you for your invaluable contribution. Without your help, this book would not have been possible.

Prologue

The world is changing faster than ever before. Technology is advancing exponentially, and our understanding of the universe is rapidly evolving. We are on the brink of a new era of discovery, where we will have access to unimaginable capabilities and knowledge.

We are entering the Metaverse—an interconnected virtual reality space without limits to our exploration. This space manifests our collective imagination, a place to explore, create, and innovate.

In the Metaverse, we will have the opportunity to develop new ways of thinking, interacting, and living. We can access new sources of information and explore new possibilities. We will be able to expand our horizons and push the boundaries of our understanding.

The Metaverse Manifesto is a set of guiding principles and values to guide us on our journey into this new world. This Manifesto is a tool to help us navigate the Metaverse, to explore its potential, and to make sure we create the best possible experience for everyone.

The Metaverse Manifesto is a call to action. We must come together to explore, learn, and create the Metaverse. We must recognize the potential of the Metaverse and use it to create a world that is more equitable, accessible, and sustainable for all.

Let us embark on this journey together and make the Metaverse our own.

Introduction

Metaverse Manifesto is a comprehensive guide to the world of digital technologies and how they can be used to create immersive experiences. It is a manifesto that advocates for the use of virtual and augmented reality, artificial intelligence, machine learning, and other cutting-edge technologies to create a shared, digital universe. It is a call to action for developers, designers, and entrepreneurs to become a part of the future of the internet and shape the next evolution of virtual reality. This book will provide an overview of the emerging technologies that are driving the Metaverse and explore their potential for creating engaging experiences. It will also discuss the challenges and opportunities of building an interconnected digital world, and how to make it a reality. Finally, it will offer insight into the economic and social implications of the Metaverse and how these technologies can be used to benefit both businesses and individuals.

CHAPTER ONE

What is the Metaverse?

The metaverse is a shared, virtual world with its own rules and laws. It's the ultimate virtual playground where people can explore, create, and connect. The metaverse is an ever-growing digital universe driven by creativity and collaboration.

At its core, the metaverse is an online space where people can connect and interact in various ways. It's a place where people can express themselves, explore new ideas, and build relationships with others. In the metaverse, anything is possible. There are no limits to what can be done or created.

A metaverse is a powerful social connection, creativity, and expression tool. It's a place where people can come together and build new relationships, explore new ideas, and create new experiences. It's an opportunity for people to come together and share their ideas, passions, and dreams.

The metaverse is a constantly evolving space. It's a place where people can create and explore new worlds, invent new technologies, and push the boundaries of what's possible. It's a place where people can come together to build a better future.

The metaverse is an open platform for exploration, expression, and collaboration. It's where people can come together and share their ideas, passions, and dreams. It's a place where anything is possible. It's a place for people to come together to create and explore new worlds, invent new technologies, and push the boundaries of what's possible.

CHAPTER TWO

The History of the Metaverse

The concept of a metaverse has been around since the mid-1980s, when pioneering computer scientist and virtual reality enthusiast Jaron Lanier coined the term. Lanier envisioned a "synthetic universe" that would be a place where people could interact in a virtual world, and he believed this would revolutionize the way people interact with each other and with computers.

The idea of a metaverse has been used in a variety of ways over the years, but it has only recently become a popular concept in the world of technology. The rise of virtual worlds such as Second Life and the increasing presence of virtual reality technology has given the metaverse a new level of visibility and relevance.

Today, many view the metaverse as a sort of "parallel universe" that exists alongside the physical world. It is a place where people can interact with others, create and explore, and engage in activities without real-world implications. This allows people to take part in activities and experiences that wouldn't be possible in the physical world, such as playing games, creating art, and even creating virtual businesses.

The potential of the metaverse is vast, and its implications for the future of technology and human interaction are only beginning to be explored. As technology and infrastructure develop, we can expect to see the metaverse become an increasingly important part of our lives. The Metaverse Manifesto seeks to explore and explain the potential, implications, and possibilities of the metaverse and how it can be used to shape the future.

The Technology Behind the Metaverse

The metaverse is a collective virtual shared space, created by the convergence of virtually enhanced physical reality and artificially simulated reality. It is an immersive, interactive, and interconnected virtual world, created and sustained by a diverse group of participants. It is an ever-evolving environment that allows for digital collaboration and exploration across a variety of digital platforms. The metaverse is the future of digital interaction, and the technology behind it is constantly advancing.

The Technology Behind the Metaverse

In order to understand the technology behind the metaverse, one must first understand its core components. The metaverse is composed of three main components: servers, clients, and users.

Servers are the backbone of the metaverse, responsible for hosting the virtual world. They must be powerful and reliable enough to handle the immense amount of data and calculations required for the metaverse to function. Servers are typically hosted in data centers and are managed by a centralized provider. Clients are the software used by users to access the metaverse.

Clients are typically desktop or mobile applications that allow users to interact with the virtual environment. Clients must be able to handle the immense amount of data and calculations required to render the metaverse in real-time.

Users are the individuals who interact with the metaverse. They can create and explore virtual spaces, communicate with other users, and develop content for the virtual world.

A variety of software and hardware powers the technology behind the metaverse. Virtual reality technology, such as head-mounted displays, motion trackers, and haptic feedback devices, are used to create immersive virtual environments. Artificial intelligence and machine learning algorithms are used to power the virtual world, allowing for complex interactions between users and virtual objects. Augmented reality technologies, such as augmented reality glasses, are used to overlay virtual objects onto the physical world. Blockchain technology is used to securely store user data and facilitate transactions within the metaverse.

Conclusion

The technology behind the metaverse is constantly evolving, allowing for new and exciting ways to interact with the virtual world. As the technology advances, the metaverse will become increasingly immersive, interactive, and interconnected. It is an ever-evolving environment that will continue to provide opportunities for digital collaboration and exploration across a variety of digital platforms.

CHAPTER FOUR

How the Metaverse is Used

In recent years, the metaverse has been used in a variety of ways. It has become an integral part of how people interact and how businesses operate, as well as being an important way to express creativity and build relationships.

One way the metaverse is used is for virtual events. Companies have used virtual events to host meetings, conferences, and other gatherings with people from all over the world. These events are often held in the metaverse, which allows people to interact in a virtual environment. This has allowed for larger events than ever before, as well as making it easier for people to attend without needing to travel.

The metaverse has also become a popular platform for gaming. Video games have been around for decades, but the metaverse has allowed for entirely new types of gaming experiences. These experiences are often highly immersive, allowing gamers to explore virtual worlds with amazing graphics and sound.

The metaverse has also been used to create virtual workspaces. Employees of companies can use the metaverse to collaborate on projects and share ideas. This has been especially useful during the pandemic, when many companies have had to switch to remote work and needed a way to stay connected.

Finally, the metaverse has been used as a platform for art and creativity. People have used the metaverse to create virtual galleries, display their artwork, and even hold virtual performances. This has allowed artists to reach a much wider audience than ever before.

The metaverse is continuing to evolve and become more popular. As more people become aware of its potential, the uses of the metaverse will continue to expand. The metaverse is sure to be an important part of our future, and the possibilities for what it can be used for are virtually limitless.

CHAPTER FIVE

Security and Privacy in the Metaverse

The Metaverse is an ever-expanding digital world, and with this growth comes an increased need for security and privacy. While the Metaverse is a new and innovative technology, it is still vulnerable to the same threats as any other online platform. It is important to be aware of the potential risks of entering the Metaverse and to take steps to protect yourself, your data, and your identity.

In the Metaverse, security is a shared responsibility between the user and the platform. Many Metaverse platforms offer security features, such as encryption and authentication, to protect user data and transactions from malicious actors. It is important to understand these security measures and use them appropriately. Additionally, users should exercise caution when sharing personal information and be aware of the potential for data breaches and other risks.

Privacy is also an important concern in the Metaverse. As with other online services, Metaverse platforms collect and store data about their users. This data can be used for a variety of purposes, including targeted advertising, analytics, and data mining. It is important to understand the privacy policies of the Metaverse platform you are using, and to ensure that your personal data is safe and secure. Additionally, it is important to be aware of the potential for data misuse and the potential for your data to be shared with third parties.

Finally, it is important to be aware of the Metaverse's potential misuse. While the Metaverse can be used for various legitimate purposes, it can also be used for illegal and unethical activities, such as fraud, identity theft, and cybercrime. It is important to be aware of these potential risks and to protect yourself and your data.

Security and privacy in the Metaverse is a complex and ever-evolving issues. As the Metaverse continues to grow, it is important to stay informed about the latest security and privacy measures and to take steps to protect yourself and your data. By understanding the potential risks and taking steps to ensure your safety, you can ensure that your experience in the Metaverse is secure and enjoyable.

The Future of the Metaverse

The future of the metaverse is bright, with many potential applications and opportunities to explore. The world of virtual reality, augmented reality, and other forms of immersive technology is rapidly evolving, and new ways of interacting with the metaverse are being created every day. With the advent of virtual reality and augmented reality, the possibilities are virtually limitless.

As technology advances, the metaverse will become increasingly more accessible and user-friendly. Virtual reality headsets are becoming more affordable, and are being developed to provide more immersive experiences. Augmented reality is being used to create more interactive experiences, with technology like Microsoft HoloLens and Magic Leap One, and more companies are entering the space.

Additionally, artificial intelligence and machine learning are becoming increasingly prevalent in the metaverse. AI and ML can be used to create more realistic and interactive virtual environments, as well as providing tools to assist in the development of new applications and experiences.

The metaverse is also becoming more socially connected, as more people are using social networks like Facebook and Twitter to engage with the metaverse. Additionally, virtual reality is being used to create more realistic and interactive virtual events and meetings, such as those held within the popular virtual world Second Life.

Finally, the metaverse is being utilized for educational purposes, as more universities and educational institutions are utilizing virtual reality for teaching, training, and research. The metaverse provides an opportunity for students to explore and engage with a virtual world, as well as providing a platform for teachers to create more immersive and interactive educational experiences.

The metaverse is constantly evolving, and the future of the metaverse is bright. With the continued advancement of technology, the metaverse will continue to provide opportunities for innovation and exploration, and will continue to be a powerful force in the way we interact with the world.

Conclusion

The Metaverse Manifesto has been a journey of exploration and discovery, uncovering the potential of the metaverse to revolutionize the way we interact with each other and with the world around us. We have discussed the potential for the metaverse to create immersive and engaging virtual experiences, as well as to enable real-time collaboration and creative exploration. We have also examined the ethical and legal implications of the metaverse, as well as its potential for education, entertainment, and commerce.

Ultimately, the metaverse is a new and exciting world of possibilities, and in order to realize its full potential, we must continue to push the boundaries of our imagination and explore the possibilities. It is our hope that this manifesto has helped to bring the metaverse to life, and to inspire further exploration and development.

The future of the metaverse is yet to be written, but the possibilities are limitless. We invite you to join us in this journey and to discover the potential of the metaverse.

References

1. Barfield, W. (2013). Metaverse manifesto: How to create a new reality. CreateSpace Independent Publishing Platform.

2. Castronova, E. (2008). Synthetic worlds: The business and culture of online games. University Of Chicago Press.

3. Chen, M., & Schmalz, M. (Eds.). (2013). Virtual reality: Simulating and enhancing the world with computers. Morgan & Claypool Publishers.

4. Damer, B. (2009). Avatars! Exploring and building virtual worlds on the Internet. Peachpit Press.

5. Davis, M. (2009). The vision of a living world: The nature of order, book 3: A process of self-organization. Center for Ecological Economics University of California, Davis.

6. Eglash, R. (2006). African fractals: Modern computing and indigenous design. Rutgers University Press.

7. Hollan, J. (Ed.). (2007). Experiences with technology: Activities and ideas for integrating technology into the classroom. Pembroke Publishers.

8. Jones, S. (2011). The metaverselle: A manifesto for a new, global, virtual culture. CreateSpace Independent Publishing Platform.

9. Rheingold, H. (1991). Virtual reality. Simon & Schuster.

10. Stone, A. R. (Ed.). (2001). The evolution of human societies: From foraging group to agrarian state. Stanford University Press.